THE LiTTLE BOOK
OF

Pocket Spells

THE LITTLE BOOK
OF

Pocket Spells

EVERYDAY MAGIC FOR THE MODERN WITCH

AKASHA MOON

Andrews McMeel
PUBLISHING®

introduction

How wonderful it is to know that interest in the craft has continued to grow since this little book was first published! Fifteen years later, I am delighted to add a sprinkling of new spells and ideas to this new edition. I hope it will continue to stoke the imaginations of its readers, encourage respect and care for our beautiful planet, as well as further exploration of folklore and living magick.

Small as it may be (and sometimes humorous), this book is in fact a condensation of decades spent studying witchcraft. You will find in its pages tried-and-tested techniques: some traditional, others my own, though based on much older magicks. Whether you wish to bless a person, win their heart, or protect your homestead, read on. If your correspondences are correct, your willpower stoked, and the universe willing, you can spell all sorts of wonderful things into your life.

AKASHA MOON, 2017

MAGICK NAME

Create a magickal persona for yourself by choosing a name that inspires you. It is common practice in magick and spellcraft to use ancient, powerful appellations. Such names attract concomitant energies (so pick carefully!) and assist in elevating the practitioner from mundane associations.

Goddess names work well, with perhaps an appending phrase that sums up your associations. An intuitive person with a love of ancient Egypt, who enjoys self-expression through movement and has additional fiery affiliations, might call herself Isis Firedancer, for example.

THE WHEEL OF LIFE

Witches and magickians ride the tide of the seasons and employ the dates of the ancient festivities for particular purposes, as follows:

★ **SAMHAIN** (October 31): To access and process issues from the past; also for divination, purification

★ **WINTER SOLSTICE/YULE** (December 21): To celebrate and nurture the life force, take stock, and make long-term plans

★ **IMBOLC** (February 2): To welcome the oncoming light born of the winter darkness

★ **SPRING EQUINOX** (March 21): For boundless energy; for facilitating a complete change in your life

★ **BELTANE** (May 1): For energy, new ideas, and sexuality

★ **SUMMER SOLSTICE** (June 21): For relating the mystical to the physical; for enlightenment, working on new levels

★ **LAMMAS/LUGHNASADH** (August 1): For celebrating the harvest of past efforts, reflecting on industry, replenishment

★ **MABON/AUTUMN EQUINOX** (September 21): For temperance, stoicism, balance, altering tides of fortune

DON'T BE DATED

The major sabbats are seasonal rather than calendar events. The celebrations are from the Celtic realms and apply to the natural world. Specific dates such as May 1 or October 31 can be useful for group get-togethers, but their accuracy is far from assured.

Celebrate the sabbats when you actually see and feel them happening. For example, is the hawthorn blossoming yet? Is it lambing season? Can you detect the pulse and flow of nature as it withdraws into the earth or as it arises in spring? Lunar tides and astrological considerations are also key. Let nature be your diary in such matters.

AURIC FACIAL

The aura is the energy field that surrounds every object. Our individual auras influence and are influenced by our physical bodies.

To give yourself an auric face-lift that diminishes wrinkles on this plane, rub your hands together, palm to palm, then separate them, palms facing each other. Move your hands together and apart a little. You should feel your aura's energy building up. Now, with light upward movements, keeping your hands about two inches from your face (or however far you wish yet without losing the energy), stroke your face's aura. It is rather like slowly splashing your face with water. Repeat as often as you like. Daily is best.

VISUALIZATION FOR EFFERVESCENCE

If you are feeling lackluster but need to be the life and soul, or at least to entertain, imagine that your aura is made out of pink champagne. Watch it weave and bubble about all those around you, the most decadent of Jacuzzis in which all become enlivened, their own auras tingling in response.

Done properly, this visualization is guaranteed to tickle the fancies of all concerned and give rise to a sparkling and fun-filled event.

LUNAR TIDES

Every lunar cycle is an opportunity to implement change, culminating in the celebration of the full moon. Phases should be employed sympathetically, as follows:

★ **NEW MOON:** To initiate or augment projects, practical endeavors

★ **WAXING MOON:** To develop ideas and spells. Daily and with a view of the moon is best. As the moon waxes, so do your fortunes

★ **FULL MOON:** To bring a cycle of growth to fruition, and to give thanks

★ **WANING MOON:** To corrode negative influences

★ **DARK MOON:** To destroy obstacles, turn negatives into creativity; for self-exploration

ENCOURAGING WEALTH

For prosperity, add silver coins to your
bath when the moon is waxing. As you splash
around, envisage yourself with enough
material wealth to allow you to enjoy life
and express your potential
to the full.

RIDING THE TIDES

In the Western Hemisphere, seasonal tides may be employed as follows:

★ **DECEMBER 21–MARCH 20:** Getting rid of what is obsolete in your life, forming solid foundations

★ **MARCH 21–JUNE 20:** Setting plans into action, initiating new schemes

★ **JUNE 21–SEPTEMBER 20:** Developing ideas, enjoying the fruits of past labor

★ **SEPTEMBER 21–DECEMBER 20:** Taking stock of patterns of progress to date; formulating, innovating

Get it Write

Writing your aim or desire down is one of the most simple and effective methods of focusing your willpower and magick. Use a special ink or pen and paper, or keep a special blank book dedicated to your purposes.

Do your scribing ritually—by moon or candlelight, for example, or within a Circle, if the muse strikes. Once you've written down what you want, don't look at it again until it's come to pass.

Get creative with your aims by writing a story in which the thing you desire happens, either literally or symbolically. So long as you're in the magickal zone, the etheric blueprint created by the process can help channel the events into reality. Truth and fiction mingle in the weirdest of ways!

CANDLE MAGICK

Candles may be used to facilitate many types of magick. Colors are significant, both traditionally and personally; they help create a conducive mood. Here are a few examples of the colors and their usage:

★ **BLUE:** For calm and study

★ **RED:** For love and passion

★ **PINK:** For fun and compassion

★ **GREEN:** For new beginnings and initiating projects

★ **YELLOW:** For wealth, health, and happiness

PURIFICATION BATH

Had an unpleasant experience? A handful of salt in the bathwater will cleanse you. Visualize it glowing blue-white and, as you enter the water, "see" your astral body being purified. At the end, envisage the negative effects of the experience spiraling away down the drain.

ALL-PURPOSE
MAGICKAL CIRCLE

A Circle brings enhanced spiritual experience and instant protection. To cast one anywhere, even on the bus to work, all you have to know is which direction you are facing. With yourself at the center, visualize to the

★ **EAST:** Yellow light, Air

★ **SOUTH:** Red light, Fire

★ **WEST:** Blue light, Water

★ **NORTH:** Green light, Earth

Imagine all negativity bouncing off the outside of your sphere, and your mind now free to connect with uncontaminated, higher realms.

FOCUSING
CANDLE MAGICK

To "magnetize" a candle, dip your thumb and forefinger in an oil relevant to your cause, or in an all-purpose "magnetizing oil," and rub from the center of the candle's stem to the tip, then from the center to the base, many times, envisaging the purpose of your spell being realized.

SiMPLE SPELL
FOR LOVE

To entrance another, work on the first Friday of a new moon. Write the person's full name in red ink on a piece of paper, and burn it in the flame of a red magnetized candle (use tweezers!).

Now say:

[The full name], if you be free and willing, come thee to me, the living embodiment of Aphrodite.

(If you are male, say:
As the living embodiment of Aphrodite.)

Repeat at the same time every Friday until the moon is full.

USE YOUR LOAF

Baking bread is both primal and powerful—and perfect hearth magick. Olive oil and sea salt may be consecrated and used in the recipe.

To bless a home, include rosemary (preferably from your own herb garden). To bless a friendship, gift the bread to the party in question on a sabbat. To enchant a lover, include cinnamon, brown sugar, and a few drops of rose water, then plait the dough and share the bun or loaf with them while still warm. This can be adjusted to any purpose through corresponding ingredients. All plants have their planetary and astrological correspondences.

☉ℿ

Om, or *Aum*, is one of the simplest and
most magickal doorways in existence.
Try meditating on it, vibrating it throughout
your body. It empowers, cleanses, and
intensifies spiritual aspiration. *Om* is literally
a gateway between worlds. Frequent
practice and concentration will
bring remarkable results.

WORDS OF POWER

The words used in a spell are of the utmost importance. Some witches and magickians use specific alphabets such as Enochian (created by Dr. John Dee, the Elizabethan astrologer, and said to be the language of angels), to enhance their work. Often, written spells are translated into runes or other scripts. The concentration involved helps imprint the intent on the subconscious.

Simplicity is of the essence in magick. Words should be chosen with care; it is always important to avoid ambivalence in spellcraft. Naive rhymes have a stronger effect than complex ritual incantations, and repetition during visualization is a key to success.

At the end of clearly stating an aim, the witch adds:

An' it harm none.
So mote it be!

Better no result than the creation of bad repercussions, which are believed in Wicca to return threefold.

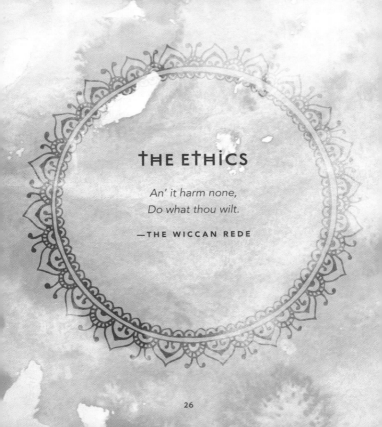

THE ETHICS

An' it harm none,
Do what thou wilt.

—THE WICCAN REDE

I CAN'T BELIEVE
IT'S MONDAY AGAIN!

Monday is, of course, sacred to the moon. Despite
the hassle of another working week, on Monday the
witch finds time to optimize the planetary influence
most pertinent to witchcraft. Purification, psychism,
magickal enhancement, and healing spells are all
performed on Mondays. Of course, the phase of the
moon is also significant. Corresponding incenses and
oils include chamomile, eucalyptus, jasmine, and
lemon. Candles should be silver, white, or indigo.

MARTIAN CONTACT

Tuesday is ruled by Mars, which makes it the right day for spells for strength, courage, facing challenges, and overcoming obstacles. Oils used in such workings include ginger, High John the Conqueror, and basil. Colors for candles are red and deep orange.

WORDS ABOUT WEDNESDAY

Because Wednesday is ruled by Mercury, the emphasis is on communication, swiftness, precision, transportation and travel, and study. Concentration and accuracy should be produced by a spell or meditation performed on this day, so it's perfect for intellectual work or magickal pursuits concerning words, magickal alphabets, and teaching. Tuesday is also relevant to computing, now the main medium of many witches! Lily of the valley, lemongrass, and clover are all suitable scents or oils. Candles should be yellow.

JOVIAL INFLUENCES

To induce friendship and companionship, to aid
family concord, and to bring luck and prosperity,
work on a Thursday. Suitable oils and incenses
include clove, honeysuckle, nutmeg, and sage.
Colors include gold, green, and royal purple.
Jupiter's influence brings generosity and warmth to
any magickal procedure and is beneficial to any
project involving expansion.

THANK THE GODDESS IT'S FRIDAY

As well as bringing the working week to a close, Venus's day graces us with delicious celestial influences. Friday is the day to cast spells for love, beauty, friendship, and passion. Candles should be green, red, or pink, the mood sensual, and the scents musky, flowery, or fruity, such as frangipani, rose, or raspberry. A long soak in a magickal bath surrounded by candles will bring extra happiness and beneficial influences to your workings.

SATURDAY'S SPELLS

Use Saturn's day to aid work within a particular structure or hierarchy. Though most people use it simply to shop and relax, Saturday will bring rewards to those who apply themselves on it. Career, property, and ambition are highlighted, so magick and mental effort will pay off. Saturday is also good for casting banishing spells. Cypress and patchouli are among the scents appropriate to Saturn; candles should be purple, black, white, or green, depending on your purpose.

SUNDAY SPELLS
SPIRITUALITY

The seventh day is the ideal time to tune in to the spiritual and mystical side of your nature. Burning frankincense, and gold and orange candles, will help attune you to the wealth of spiritual knowledge waiting to harmonize your life. This is also a propitious time for healing and creative work.

TO LIFT THE BLUES

Orange oil is powerfully uplifting. Evaporating some, or using a few drops in the bath, will help dissipate the blues. For added clout, use an orange candle in conjunction. Several candles placed around the bath as you soak will lift your spirits.

If you are in a more ritualistic mode, place six candles around the room so that you stand in a circle of light. Imagine an equilateral cross at your solar plexus. If it seems to waver or be imbalanced, invest energy into keeping it still and upright. (This cross represents your centeredness in the Universe.)

Finally, imagine a stream of orange-yellow light pouring into you. The candle flames are foci for this force. Wrap the light of the flames around yourself until you are "cloaked" in an astral raiment. Return to your workaday life as a rejuvenated Child of Light.

incense tip

Loose incenses are perfect accompaniments to spells, allowing you to select the right herbs, gums, and woods according to their correspondences. However, the charcoal disks on which they are burned often spit and create a terrible smog. To avoid this, light the disk and leave it to smolder somewhere safe for twenty minutes before sprinkling the incense.

REJUVENATION BATH

This spell works best using a real emerald, so buy or borrow one for the best effect.

Put the emerald in the bath (make sure the plug is in!) in about five inches of lukewarm to cold water. Allow it to soak for at least one hour. Remove the emerald and add warm to hot water.

Sprinkle with seven drops of basil, thyme, or lavender essential oils (if you are pregnant, use a diluted form, such as scented bubble bath). When you are immersed, rest the emerald on your sternum, at the heart chakra (one of the seven major energy points of the body and aura).

Envisage its brilliant green rejuvenation energy permeating the water and you. Do not arise until every cell in your body has been aurically saturated in this way.

WATERFRONT SPELL I

To bring rewarding adventures into your life, find a fallen twig that appeals to you. You can correspond the wood to your aim by deciding which planet is appropriate to your intent (Jupiter for prosperity and expansion, for example) and finding a tree ruled by it. (Nutmeg is one such for Jupiter.) It is best not to take your twig directly from the tree, but if you have no choice, be modest and say please and thank you to the Dryad, the spirit of the tree.

Whittle your small twig into a wand while concentrating on the adventures and rewards you wish for.

On the day of a new moon, take the magick wand to a river or the sea (never an enclosed body of water such as a lake!), concentrate hard on what you wish for, stating it out loud if desired and possible, and throw the wand as far out as you can manage. Visualize the energies you have sent flowing out into the Universe, to return, eventually, laden with exotic possibilities.

WATERFRONT SPELL 2

To rid yourself of unwanted energies, take a handful of soil and concentrate into it thoughts of what you wish to shed. When you are satisfied that your thoughts have imbued the soil, place it in a permeable pouch made of a material such as cheesecloth and, as you tie it, visualize these undesirable influences as now being cut off from your life.

When the moon is waning or dark, take the pouch (during the day is fine) to an open waterfront and hurl it in. As the water saturates it, it is cleansed, and as it is carried away from you, so are the unwanted influences removed from your life.

BATHTIME BREW

Dried herbs in the bath will imbue you with their special properties and make the steam refreshing and cleansing. Experiment with different shrubs and combinations.

Favorites include:

★ **ROSEMARY** for confidence

★ **THYME** for creativity and strength in your own convictions

★ **LAVENDER** to refresh and brace

★ **SAGE** for love, stimulation, and cleanliness, and for dispelling infections such as colds

Note: Herbs should always be used with caution, especially when pregnant.

GRIS GRIS

If somebody is giving you grief, either magickally or psychologically, you can shield yourself from his or her influence with the following technique.

Write the name in black at the center of a thick piece of paper.

Fold it up, starting by creasing it across the name.

Keep folding, imagining the person's power diminishing, until you have the smallest possible capsule of paper. Now burn it somewhere from which you can later retrieve the ash, saying:

Your power is dying;
I cancel thee out.
[Name], I cancel thee out.

Repeat this statement as many times as required to facilitate a strong mental image of you doing just what it says.

When all the embers have died, carefully collect the remains and store them in a black silk scarf or pouch, preferably with a sample of the person's hair or some nail clippings.

This mixture can be used as a base for further antidote processes.

ANTIDOTE I

The best antidote in the world is to ignore your aggressor—and literally not give him or her a second thought. Antipathy builds up very strong links.

If these links are already established, one way to diminish them is to take a salt bath. While soaking, imagine the cords that connect you and X dissolving in the bright, cleansing light of the salt water.

When you emerge from the bath, pull the plug, and as the water drains from the tub, sprinkle in the ash produced in the preceding gris gris spell, and visualize it effervescing white light and dissolving. Then watch it go down the drain on this plane. Make sure none of it remains in the tub.

This simple technique works for many problems, because it eliminates unwanted influences. Performing it with the waning or dark moon will help for ridding, with the new moon for new beginnings and growing inner strength.

ANTIDOTE 2

Take a pinch of the ash from the gris gris process on page 42 and mix it with some banishing (or cleansing) oil. Take a black candle and anoint it from the center to both ends, mentally imbuing it with your feelings of antipathy for the person concerned. When the moon is just beginning to wane, light it. As the wax melts, so will the person's hostile influence on you. Repeat daily until the dark moon.

CURE FOR FORGETFULNESS

Drunk daily, this simple potion will help
revive flagging brain cells. Take a large pinch
of dried rosemary and the same of dried sage.
Add boiling water and steep for at least
five minutes. If you remember to drink
this as often as possible, you're
on your way!

ANTIDOTE 3

If you are faced with a persistent problem person, try the following. Take the rest of the gris gris ash (or make more, which you may need to do if you have already worked the preceding spells—see page 42) and, by the light of a waning moon and working on a Saturday, mix it with a little St. John's wort. This herb is active against evil and helps to protect and purify.

Standing over the mixture, chant: "By the power of Saturn, I cast thee out!" while strongly envisioning your aggressor losing grip on your psyche and well-being.

If the person is particularly tenacious, you might like to burn the resultant mixture in a ritual of your own device (always the best sort). Each cleansing by fire will loosen the aggressor's influence.

Then, wear a little St. John's wort in a pouch around your neck. Alternatively, wear the entire original mixture in a pouch.

ASTRAL
AIR FRESHENER I

Garlic has a reputation for banishing vampires
(though most vampires I know love garlic!).
However, it does absorb negative energy, so if there
are bad vibes in your house, leaving peeled cloves
of garlic, slightly nicked, around the place will help.
These must be removed or replaced every twenty-
four hours.

ASTRAL
AIR FRESHENER 2

This method may stink a little on the material planes, but it has been used for centuries to clear negative energies. Simply place a cut onion in the vicinity that needs cleansing. The evil influences will be drawn to it and get caught in its numerous layers. Throw the onion out and replace, if necessary, every twenty-four hours.

SLEEP WELL

To ensure that a dear departed is "asleep" to this realm (i.e., is progressing spiritually rather than being caught up with the trivial or emotional issues of his or her last life), light a small, white candle (preferably on the anniversary of the death), and burn a little dried herb incense as you work.

Meditate on the fact that emotional and spiritual bonds endure but that specific circumstances change. Send your love to the soul concerned, perhaps with a few words of peaceful encouragement. Do not be selfish and hold your loved one back with sentiment. Imagine him or her liberated from all worldly concerns.

Now envisage a thick curtain descending between you. That is the way it should be, for now. Let the incense out the window and extinguish the candle.

MARITAL BLISS

A crystal bowl containing rose water, on which seven drops of essential rose oil are placed, will keep a marriage sweet. Put it in the bedroom. If it needs a boost, add fresh rose petals. However, never allow the petals to decay. The fresher the water, the more blissful the union.

ALL NIGHT LONG

Aphrodisiacs have to be among the world's most used enchantments. There are literally thousands available, and all cultures have them. The following is a relatively gentle spell!

Take a teaspoon of cinnamon and add to it seven drops of essential rose oil. Boil up a small pan of lovage leaves (dried lovage is fine) in a cup of water for five minutes. Leave it to steep for another two. Add one tablespoon of this concoction to the previous ingredients (use the remaining lovage potion for your pre-all-night bath!). As you do so, contemplate the pleasures you intend to enjoy.

Leave the mixture out to dry—beneath the sun is best. Finally, when the mixture has returned to powder, sprinkle it lightly on the bed you wish to bless.

BLESSIɳG FOOD

For real nourishment on every plane, psychically
enhance your food by holding your hands over it
and mentally (or verbally, if at home) reciting a small
prayer or mantra of thankfulness. As you do so,
visualize positive energy pouring from the Universe
into your hands, then being directed into the food
before you.

ARABIAN NIGHTS

This spell is best performed on a Friday. To attract as many friends and lovers as your heart desires, take nine drops from a phial of jasmine oil, preferably with some real jasmine or lilac flowers in the bowl, and add to it a spoonful of rose water.

Stand with your hands over the sweet-smelling combination, and concentrate pink light into the bowl. See the potion glowing with attractive, fun energies.

Dab a little behind your ears and on your wrists before you go out. Be aware of the pink light, concentrated at your pulse points, coloring your entire aura. Now, enjoy!

ASTRAL TRAVEL

To facilitate astral travel, envisage yourself, when on the verge of sleep, traveling toward a huge silver-white moon set in an indigo sky. As you drift off, try to pass into the orb—and beyond it. Burning a little jasmine incense, or placing a (preferably silver or indigo) cloth with nine drops of the oil on it under your pillow will also aid astral projection.

FAST GOOD LUCK

The Wheel of Fortune is always turning. Every individual receives his or her quota of circumstances, both good and bad, throughout the course of his or her incarnations. If you are undergoing a run of bad luck, it is because there is something you need to learn—an attitude perhaps that needs to be processed, or the effect of actions past that need to be nullified (usually involving some discomfort).

However, the key point in all of these issues is to strive. To encourage the Wheel of Fortune to carry you upward again, visualize yourself on the Wheel, at whatever point you believe yourself to be. With all the mental and spiritual energy you can muster, make the Wheel rotate so that it carries you skyward. Be sure to do this clockwise, or you will take a dip before you ascend! Repeat daily until luck is working in your favor again.

LUCKY LODESTONE

Clove oil is renowned for attracting power and good luck. However, it is rather irritating to the skin, so, rather than wearing it, anoint a small magnet while beseeching the gods to look upon you kindly. The most relevant to this spell is Hermes, who brought sudden windfalls to the ancient Greeks. The Hindu goddess Laksmi is also connected with prosperity and good luck. Use a deity you feel a rapport with. When you receive inner acknowledgment that your request has been granted, wrap the magnet in bright yellow silk and carry it with you at all times. The unexpected should become a delight after this!

TO KEEP YOUR LOVER FAITHFUL

Take a small, unwashed garment that belongs to your partner. Hold it, and contemplate your intimacy, the sacredness of your union (despite the grubby garment!), and the shared times to come.

Place it before you, take some wintergreen oil, and, while looking at the oil, mentally block out all potential assailants of your partnership. See barriers come down between your lover and any interlopers.

Lightly sprinkle the garment with your oil, saying:

Be it night or be it day,
You shall never wish to stray!

Keep the garment in your possession for at least seven days. After that, you can leave it somewhere for your lover to find.

If you ever get a frisson of discomfort with regard to potential infidelity, dab a little of the oil onto yourself. If your partner seems to be straying anyway, bring those mental barriers down around you again.

Repeat as necessary, but be sensible. Sometimes the tides change, and it is best to let go.

CONCENTRATION

Rosemary is renowned in herbal lore as a concentration aid. While working, evaporate the oil to keep yourself focused. Dried leaves can also be steeped in boiling water and drunk as tea. My personal favorite is to keep a rosemary plant close to where you work. A gentle rub of the leaves releases a magickal, refreshing fragrance ideal to help you focus.

PSYCHIC BEVERAGES

The liquids we put into our bodies are also psychically relevant.

Water purifies on all levels. Tea and coffee aid with determination and creativity. Red wine is symbolic of the blood of Life. Herb teas, of course, have numerous properties. Color is as important as content, especially in visualization.

Thus, any solid or liquid is potentially a spell.

FORTIFIED CIDER

Because of its deep golden color and its origin in apples, cider is a great carrier for health visualizations. Only one small glass per spell, mind!

Take a modest measure of sweet cider. Drop a tigereye gem into it. Light a yellow candle and place it behind the glass, so that you can see the flame through the liquid.

Envisage healthful light streaming into the candle, its focus point the flame. As the flame illuminates the golden-orange brew, visualize this vibrancy being transferred into the cider. Keep this visualization up for as long as you are able.

When finished, slowly drink the cider (beware the tigereye!). With each sip, feel light and health entering your body, driving out any unwanted "dark" patches. By the end of the glass, your astral body should be literally glowing with health!

CHAKRIC NUTRIENTS

Food can be used for psychic purposes, to enhance visualization, and to strengthen the astral body through their colors.

Green foods strengthen the heart chakra (or energy point), red foods aid with determination, and yellow-orange foods such as squash and mango help to build up emotional strength and independence, courtesy of the solar plexus chakra. Meals can be concocted to aid any spell or visualization.

ᛏROUBLESOME COWORKER OR BOSS

If you are being dealt with unfairly by a peer or authority figure, work on a Thursday when the moon is waxing. A little Libra incense (available from most good New Age shops) will also help with this spell.

Light a purple candle and envisage the Scales of Justice. In one pan visualize yourself, in the other the person or persons concerned. See how the scales are weighted unfairly? (They should be. If not, you might wish to reconsider your position!) So too must everybody else. Mentally magnify the scales and, if you can, visualize the relevant external parties gawking in outrage.

Now appeal to the universal Justice-makers, such as Jupiter and Maat, to tip the scales back to a position fair to you. Keep performing this exercise until the pans are in balance again.

TO GAIN EMPLOYMENT

Take a small citrine stone (often available polished from New Age stores) and concentrate orange light into it. Embalming it with a little orange oil may well aid this process. The citrine is known to enhance confidence, and orange helps with the organizational skill, self-control, and focus required at interviews. Even when writing cover letters, this simple charm can be used, kept either at your side or in a pocket. If you can find a piece of citrine through which a chain (or even a cord) can be strung, all the better— this will enable you to wear it around your neck and thus have its influence close to your chakras!

FAST MONEY

As with any augmenting spell, the following is best worked with a waxing moon. Take a gold, red, or green candle and anoint it with a little clove oil. As you light the wick, imagine money being attracted to you. Be sure to add the proviso that this is through no harm to yourself or anybody else! (Insurance money, for example, could be one of the ways for this spell to backfire if the ground rules are not set!)

Persistence pays off in magick, so if you can find the time and inspiration to repeat this spell every day until the full moon, all the better. Beginning on a Thursday will kick-start the process.

HiGHER SELF

It can be difficult to stay attuned to one's higher purpose in this workaday world, even when living with strong metaphysical beliefs.

Creating a small "sacred space" to visit every day is an effective way to counteract the mundane. This space does not have to be physical, but if you have room for an altar in a space conducive to meditation, all the better. You can embellish your space as you progress, starting with objects of significance in the past and progressing on to those relevant at present.

Alternatively, you can create an astral temple (see the following spell).

Visit your space as often as you can. Use it to attune your physical manifestation with your higher purpose. Three points to dwell on are: What am I achieving in this incarnation? What am I meant to learn from my life to date—what are the recurring themes? How can I follow my inner calling in order to make my life happy, creative, and beneficial to others?

ASTRAL TEMPLE

Recall a place that you loved, or imagine an environment that seems magickal to you. Envisage it very strongly. Now put something there. You might like to plant a shrub or tree, or to mentally place a beloved object on the spot.

Return to your sanctuary the following day. Look at whatever you placed there. If it is still like new, or is flourishing, this is a good "place" for you to come. If not, try again until you are happy with the results.

Whenever you wish to cast a spell or ponder the higher aspects of life, see and feel yourself in this place, your astral temple. The connections to your sacred space will grow as you do. You will soon find that your "imaginary" hideout has a life of its own.

KInDLY EXORCISM

If you are being blighted by a troublesome spirit, do not follow the conventional exorcism techniques, unless it is truly evil (which is highly unlikely). Conventional exorcism causes great distress to a spirit that is obviously already undergoing difficulties.

Instead, try to get a sense of its personality. Then construct an appealing mental landscape for it to inhabit. Behind this, envisage the Light of cosmic compassion and progression.

Invite the spirit into your landscape. The more vivid and appealing this is, the better.

When the spirit has "moved into" your appealing landscape, concentrate on the Light, asking the Powers That Be to take the entity on.

ANCESTRAL WORSHIP

As incarnating souls, we gravitate toward families who will teach us what we need to know. Even if our immediate family does not seem spiritually relevant (in an obvious sense), we frequently discover predecessors with the same interests and spiritual urges. It is possible to connect with those "familiar" spirits who are willing.

Sitting quietly, carry a line of light that starts at your forehead backward from the present moment through your life, with all its major events (in reverse order), until you reach the point of your birth.

Now repeat the process with the parent whose bloodline you are choosing to study. See him or her retreating in time to the point of conception. Repeat with a grandparent, great-grandparent, and so on until your thread reaches the ancestor you wish to contact.

Envisage the light connecting you both, and send your thoughts down it, as if it were a phone line. With any luck, you should receive an answer.

BLESSING A PET
THAT HAS PASSED OVER

It is heartbreaking to lose a beloved pet, even when we believe in the afterlife. Sometimes we do not get the chance to say goodbye, which makes our loss feel even worse.

Take a treat that was favored by your pet, and place it before a blue votive candle along with a photo of you together.

Light the candle, gently thinking the animal's name. When your pet appears (dogs are better at this than cats), welcome it, and mentally give it the treat. Thank it for your time together—elaborate as you wish. Explain that you realize it was your pet's time to go (otherwise the pet may not be able to move on), and wish it joyous newfound independence.

When you are finished, blow out the candle and bury the treat in your garden, or, if you have no garden, leave it in a place favored by your pet. Your pet would not begrudge another animal taking its treat now.

ANY-PURPOSE SPELL

The technique of sigilization was brought into modern magick by Austin Osman Spare. It is a simple and effective way to imprint the subconscious with a desired result.

Create a sentence that summarizes what you want. Be clear, and aim for one thing at a time. Write it down, and take the first letter of every word. If any letters are repeated, reduce them to just one. Take all the letters and create a monogram of them. It's fine for lines to overlap or be written backward. You should end up with a magickal-looking but indecipherable symbol.

When you are emotionally charged up, stare at it. No need to recall its intent—your subconscious will do that for you. The greater the energy directed at it, the bigger the end result.

SIXTH SENSES

The image produced by Kahlil Gibran in *The Prophet* of a palm with an eye in it can be employed in visualization to enhance the sixth sense.

With your eyes closed, sit opposite the person or object you wish to perceive psychically, your palms open to him; her, or it. Envisage eyes in the palms' centers, emitting rays of emerald and violet light toward your subject. Relax, and let your intuition flow.

AUTO CHILL OUT

I use this technique whenever the humdrum aspects of life and relationships are getting in the way of my spiritual integrity. It may be performed anywhere.

Imagine yourself sitting in a snowy mountain range such as the Himalayas. It is night, and a full moon shines brightly above. You are completely alone. In your hands is a crystal ball. In it are images of your life's actions. Watch the most relevant scenes play themselves out before you.

Now imagine that your life has ended, and all that is in the crystal ball is all you have achieved in that incarnation.

Assess what you wish you had done differently.

When you are ready, "transfer" yourself into the crystal ball, and put into action the principles that you could see, with your overview, that were required to make your life worthwhile.

CHILL OUT, YOU!

To cause another person to chill out, try to procure a sample of his or her handwriting, preferably produced when the person is irate. Alternatively, draw a small picture of the person as he or she appears when angry.

Fold the paper up as tightly as possible and wrap it in a little plastic wrap, saying:

Keep the fires of wrath
from spilling;
To calméd be I spell you willing!

Place the paper in an ice cube tray, and pop it into the freezer.

TO ATTRACT
AMIABLE PEOPLE

On the night of a new moon, light two
candles, one of dark green and one of
vibrant pink. Light a sweet-smelling joss stick
such as gardenia or rose. Take a photograph
of yourself with your best friends, and hold
it out to the moon. Turn it over
three times, saying:

Power of friendship, others see:
Return to me by the power
of Three!

TO ATTRACT AMIABLE SPIRITS FROM THE OTHER SIDE

Voodoo altars often feature cups of whiskey and rum to attract and thank spirits helpful to the practitioner. Any offering will bring spirits to whom such a gift appeals.

So, decide the sorts of spirits whose company you would enjoy, and make them gifts of a suitable nature; perhaps a sweet cake or something that, to you, represents enduring friendship.

On the night of a new moon, light a candle of pale green, and another of pale pink. Place them on your altar or a small table, along with a stick of sweet-smelling incense such as rose or jasmine. Say:

Accept these gifts, and Blesséd be:
Happy spirits, come to me.

Place your welcome gifts with the candles. When you perceive a spirit who suits your purpose, say:

Merry meet.

When you wish the spirit to depart (and return), say:

Merry part; and merry meet again.

PICK ME!

If you wish to be selected for a particular endeavor, take a red candle and, on the night of a full moon, anoint it with clove oil. Light the candle and think of everything that fits you to this post. Envisage yourself surrounded by vibrant red-orange light, like that created by the candle, and crackling with the "electricity" of your enthusiasm.

Re-create this light whenever you think of yourself in a position to be picked. If this involves a face-to-face encounter, dab yourself with a little clove oil on the day.

TO QUIET A GOSSIP

Perform this spell when the moon is waning.

To bind a malicious tongue, write down the full initials of its owner. Eliminate any repeated letters. Translate the remaining letters into your favorite runic or magickal script. Make a monogram of these characters, so that you are left with a figure that represents them to you. Carve this onto a small piece of wood, saying:

Though thy tongue was once so free,
Now it's wooden: one, two, three.

With each number, carve a line through the name.

Every time you hear or think of this person gossiping, visualize your runic monogram on his or her tongue.

TO QUELL A TROUBLEMAKER

Use this spell to neutralize a pesky influence without causing harm to its perpetrator.

On the night of, or after, a full moon, take a small black candle. Hold it in your hands and think of all the trouble caused by the relevant party. The candle represents this trouble.

Using a needle, carve the initials of the troublemaker into the candle. Now burn it, thinking of the trouble diminishing.

Repeat every night of the waning moon, until the candle is spent. Take the tiny bit of wax and wick that remains, and stick the needle through it. Wrap the needle and spent candle in a piece of white silk, and bury it in a graveyard.

PROTECTING A CHILD

Actions speak louder than spells when it comes to child protection, but this spell may be used to enhance whatever you are doing on the material plane.

Take a photo of the child, or a lock of his or her hair. Place it on a small square of soft yellow cloth.

Hold a shiny new penny up to the sun, and say:

One in a hundred, a hundred in one;
Give health and protection, Spiritual Sun!

Place this penny with the photo or hair.

Now add three comfrey leaves to the contents, and send a ray of love and protection into the ingredients. Tie with a white ribbon so that it becomes a pouch.

Hide this pouch in the room of the child.

DRYADIC COMFORT

Trees are one of nature's most wondrous gifts, as most people would agree. Occasionally, however, vandals rip down striplings or take branches from older trees, causing distress to the trees and the community alike.

To comfort the tree-spirit, sit down close to it, perhaps holding a branch or leaf in your hands, and attune yourself to the nature Deva (or guardian entity) in charge. This can be done by reaching out your mind and asking to connect. A slight shimmer or your intuition will tell you when you are being perceived by the spirit of the tree.

Tell the spirit how much you enjoyed it, and that you wish to donate some of your energy to help it heal. If the tree is completely ruined (as were two young blossoming cherries in my mother's village recently), thank it for the pleasure it gave you, and send energy anyway. The organic manifestation is dead, but the nature Deva is not.

ĴEALOUSY RIDDER: SELF

Work with the waning moon. Take a black candle and anoint it, from center to tip in both directions, with cypress or mimosa oil. Burn a patchouli-scented joss stick as you work.

Think about all the things you feel jealous about. Invest the candle with these energies, but don't light it! You've made the effort to break the effects of your self-pollution on the earth plane; now you're going to break them on the astral plane too.

Place the candle over a piece of green silk.

Thinking of all the reasons to rid yourself of this plague, snap the candle. Now break it up in whatever way and as much as you desire.

Collect all the pieces in the silk, and tie the bundle with a white ribbon. Chuck it wherever you chuck the other things you no longer wish to possess. Complete the effect by taking a purification bath in energized salt water.

JEALOUSY RIDDER: OTHERS

On a night of the waning moon (nearest to the full moon is best), take a black or purple candle and anoint it with cypress oil from center to tip and center to base, thinking of how the cleansing aroma of the cypress is already freshening the perceptions of your "rival."

Light the candle.

Now take three dried rose petals and, using tweezers, hold them one by one in the flame. This action is symbolic of your friendship and patience sweetening the atmosphere. Project all the positive, healing energy you can at the person, and send as much love to him or her as you can muster.

Either burn the candle down to its base, working on consecutive nights (no need to use petals and leaves again, unless you wish to), or burn it all now. Wrap any remains with a few comfrey leaves, and bury (use a biodegradable wrapper!).

GARTER OF VENUS

Every witch knows how to use a garter to her best advantage. Traditionally, garters were male vestments, as worn by the knights of that order, but they have become a female province.

Take one ready-made garter or, for extra energy, create one yourself out of three ribbons. Tie the ribbons at the top and plait them loosely nine times.

On a Friday, when the moon is waxing or full, take your garter with you into the moonlight. Hold it up to the Goddess, and contemplate the magickal enchantment it will produce when wrapped around your thigh.

Ask for the powers of seduction known to so many goddesses, ancient and modern, to be invested into your magickal apparel. Wear it on your next date.

SAGE SPELL

The American Indians used bunches of sage to cleanse the atmosphere of evil influences. This method works, but the smell can be rather overpowering.

Work at the new moon, and keep the windows open. Move from room to room with your burning sage bundle (widely available from New Age stores), and as you waft the cleansing incense around, envisage all negative entities and atmospheres fleeing through the open windows, or being dissolved by the astringent smoke.

Finally, banish the remains by waving them out. When the smoke has departed and just a faint scent remains, close your windows and mentally seal them and the doors from unwanted beings and atmospheres.

COUPLE ATTUNEMENT

To attune spiritually and psychically with your partner, sit cross-legged, face-to-face. You are going to utilize the chakra system, that is, the seven major energy points of the body and aura, which run from the base of the spine to the crown of the head.

Starting at the base chakra, imagine a line of light connecting you both. Do the same with the intestinal chakra. Continue up through the solar plexus, heart, throat, third eye, and finally the crown chakras.

Now envisage all seven major energy centers linked.

Whenever you and your partner feel you are becoming separated, for whatever reason, repeat this process. You will soon find that you are never truly apart.

MAGICKAL ENHANCEMENT

Any focused ritual repeated often
enough will boost your magickal powers.
Intent is everything in magick. Use your
intuition! A simple example is working with
the waxing moon, burning a purple votive
candle every evening, and concentrating
on the accumulation of Universal
Energy, which may be used
for any purpose.

TO STRENGTHEN A LONG-DISTANCE FRIENDSHIP

If you have a close and trusted friend who has moved abroad or to a far-flung town, you will find your time together even more precious. Buy a large notepad and, when you are together, light an orange candle over it. Together, say:

Merry meet and merry part:
Before I go, my heart I'll show.

Now, each make a dated entry in the pad. Decide on a keeper of the journal.

Every time you meet, repeat the incantation, then use the pages to explore your progress and thoughts since you last met.

I've been doing this with a witchy friend for years now, and what started off as a regular diary has become a fascinating and enlightening Book of Shadows. (Many witches record their spells in a Book of Shadows.)

Ritual and honesty cannot fail to enhance a friendship.

✝O ENHANCE A CLOSE FRIENDSHIP

Buy a pack of Tarot cards with your best friend. Pick a set that you both feel is appropriate to your joint energy.

Sitting face-to-face, take turns shuffling the cards. Concentrate on the energy you produce together as you do so. This ritual is aided by envisaging the light emanating from each of you, its cohesion, and its effect on the Tarot.

Wrap the pack in a black silk scarf.

Whenever either of you is confused or distressed, or simply in need of some guidance, get the other one to read from the pack. If you need a book at first, don't worry—it takes years to really learn the cards.

After a few tries with this ritual, you will find both your friendship and your psychic sensitivity regarding your friend greatly enhanced.

intuition

If you feel yourself lacking in the intuition department (one hopes you will be insightful enough to know!), use Mondays to meditate on the moon. Even just a small time spent contemplating the silver orb before you sleep will help. You will soon find yourself becoming attuned to the psychic wavelengths traditionally associated with that celestial body.

LINES OF LIGHT

Use this spell to pick out people who can benefit you, whatever your endeavor.

On a Thursday when the moon is waxing, light an orange candle and think of the types of people you wish to attract and how you will be of mutual benefit. Say:

If they be of use to me,
Lines of vibrant light I'll see.

When you find yourself placed before people of potential relevance, look above their heads with your intuition switched on. Those with lines of light above them are—you got it!—the people it is worth expending your energy on.

PSYCHOMANCY SPELL

Many psychics are able to pick up details of people and places from objects they handle. To develop this art, take some rock salt and hold it up to the moon when it's visible, saying:

Purify my hands and mind:
In what I touch, the truth I'll find.

Dissolve the salt in hot mineral water and wash your hands in it while visualizing bright white light purifying and imbuing your being, particularly your hands. Before you touch any object you wish to receive information from, visualize this light, and repeat the process if possible.

NULLIFYING NEGATIVITY

To diminish unwanted emotions, take a small black candle and mentally imbue it with your wrath, jealousy, insecurity, or negativity. As it burns, envisage these life-hindering energies dissipating into raw, pure silver energy. Mentally reabsorb the energy, now cleansed, and resolve to use it constructively. Be warned; its power is now redoubled!

FOLLOW ME, BOY

When neither the sun nor the moon is visible, place four drops of vervain oil in a mortar with three mistletoe berries, and crush. Visualize the symbol of Venus (☿) filling the sky as you do so, sending rays of pinkish silver light into your potion and you.

If you are after a particular man, say:

If none it harm,
Enhance my charm,

imagining him attached to you by seven strong but beautiful lines of pinkish silver light. Now visualize him, still attached, scintillated by you.

If you are simply looking for fun, imagine yourself shining like the symbol, your rays going out in many directions.

When you feel the mistletoe mush is charged, apply it immediately to your pulse points, or, if you wish to delay the effects of your spell, place it in a dark glass container and use when required.

Now say:

Follow me, boy,
and enjoy.

FOLLOW ME, GIRL

Under a full moon, and preferably when Venus is visible, slowly anoint a dried vanilla pod with seven drops of vanilla oil. Place it in a small bag with five red rose petals. As you put the petals in the pouch, imagine yourself "bagging" the girl (or a girl who matches your specifications).

Now say:

An' none it harm,
Enhance this charm.

Sprinkle the vanilla pod and rose petals with ten pinches of cinnamon, saying:

For lust and trust,
follow me, girl!
For leisure and pleasure,
follow me, girl!
For all that you treasure,
follow me, girl!

(Remember, naive verses create more effective magick precisely because of their childlike simplicity.) When you have visualized the object of your desire smilingly following you, tie the pouch with a green ribbon.

Carry your charm on a string around your neck (under your clothes, of course!) or in an upper pocket. When you wish to activate it, tap it seven times, and smile.

If she is willing on a higher level, the girl will follow.

SPIRIT FLIGHT

Need a break? Why not get out of your body? This technique may take practice, or it may occur spontaneously; either way it results in the ultimate nocturnal holiday—astral travel.

Take one purple candle and, from center to base and center to tip, anoint it with wormwood oil. If you cannot get wormwood oil, ginseng or balsam oil will suffice.

When the candle is charged, light it. Just before bed is best, but any time will do. Sit cross-legged before the candle (in the lotus posture if possible), spine straight. Shut your eyes, but still see the candle—at the level of your third eye, between and slightly above the eyebrows.

Now visualize yourself above the candle. Rise as high as you can. When you are ready, return to your body, open your eyes, and extinguish the flame. You need perform this ritual for only a few minutes every day; the key is the regularity of your desire to exit your body. Soon your spirit will fly at night.

DIVINATION BY TV

This technique was propounded in its original form by the Temple of Psychick Youth in the 1990s.

Sit in contemplation for a while, in as much silence as is possible in this day and age. Attune yourself to the Universe.

Now think of all the networks of communication that span the world—the psychic and spiritual, the electronic and technological. Meditate on the fact that everything we choose to perceive is of significance to us. Concentrate on a question you would like to ask or a theme that is of particular relevance to you at present. Ask the Universe to give you an accurate response.

Now, turn on the television (or radio) and hop channels swiftly. The images, words, and phrases received are your answers.

GROUNDING SPELL

There are times when consciousness seems like a kite stuck between conflicting currents and needs to be reeled in and grounded. If you are unable to concentrate because of others, or because of your own thoughts and emotions, this simple spell is for you.

Take a pinch of soil and a pinch of salt, and place them with a small stone in a pouch. Then, say (or think loudly) the following words while stamping on the ground with each syllable:

Salt of salt. Earth of earth.

Whenever you need to be grounded, squeeze the pouch in the palm of your hand, and repeat the words mentally ten times. This spell also works to diminish negative influences and to counteract psychic attack, should you be unfortunate enough to undergo it.

LAUNCHING A PROJECT

Buy a flowering potted geranium. Procure a picture or statue of one of the following: Ganesha, Laksmi, Apollo, St. Peter, or any other deity or intercessor you like whose auspices are good in a business sense (one may think laterally—Apollo's archery guarantees farsightedness and precision work, for example, while his solar qualities bring propitious circumstances).

Place the plant before the god-form, saying (or thinking):

May my venture prosper and
flourish like the flowers of
this plant.

Imagine golden light streaming from above the head of your celestial business partner, through his or her body, and into you.

Now light a stick of incense as a thank-you, placing it in the soil of your plant to burn. Repeat as required.

We cannot expect a potted plant to keep its flowers forever, so to avoid expiry vibes, remove the incense as soon as the flowers begin to wither. Replacement blooms are best in yellow and orange to red.

invoking the goddess

Personified female energies of the Creative Intelligence may be invoked for specific purposes. Here are some examples:

★ **The Egyptian Isis,** for magick, fertility, love

★ **Persephone,** Demeter's daughter in Greek mythology, for transcending unwanted situations

★ **Hera,** Zeus's Olympian wife, for a proactive approach to setting errant partners straight

★ **Nephthys,** sister of Isis, for inner strength and overcoming grief

A knowledge of mythology and its archetypes brings great rewards in magick, allowing the practitioner to link with established psychological and subconscious patterns.

INVOKING THE GODS

In addition to goddesses, personified god-forms can be invoked with powerful effect. Here are some examples:

★ **PAN,** the goat-footed god of Greek mythology, to break a deadlock, halt complacency, or liberate sexuality

★ **THE EGYPTIAN OSIRIS,** to emerge smiling from a situation of enmity

★ **HORUS,** son of Isis and Osiris, for balance or communication skills

★ **THOTH,** the Egyptian scribe and magickian, for academe or learning

★ **ODIN,** the Norse god who suffered to attain the runes for humankind, to help attune to a greater good

WOW!

To make your impact on a potential lover, look straight into his or her eyes (by candle- or firelight is best, but any intimate situation will do) and envisage a fishing line, complete with hook, coming out of your pupils, into your lover's, and down into his or her gut. Do your utmost to connect psychically.

Every time you think good thoughts about your lover, remember that line, and send all of your positive, sparkly energy down it.

You should prove gut-wrenchingly irresistible to your lover.

talismanic magic

There are talismans available to suit any religious proclivity. A protective rune worn around the neck is good for those who relate to the Norse gods, a hieroglyph cast in precious metal or a trusty scarab for those who prefer Egyptian lore. An equilateral cross confers balance to a Qabalist. Pick your talisman to suit your inclinations and purpose.

When you find or make it, direct brilliant blue light at it and say:

Protection to the left of me,
Protection to the right of me,
Before me, behind me,
Over me, under me.
So mote it be.

Charge your talisman with extra energy to meet particular challenges as they occur.

HOLiSTiC BOOST

For self-confidence, carry a sprig of fresh rosemary with you. When you need strength and refreshment, rub it between your thumb and forefinger. This is also a good remedy for headaches, neuralgia, hypertension, and unwanted influences.

LIGHT OF INTUITION

At the full moon, take an overview of your life. Are you heading in the direction you want to? Is your life path fulfilling, progressive, and fun? By meditating by the light of the lunar orb, particularly with the aid of a trusty Tarot pack and a Book of Shadows (your magickal diary), you will gain enhanced perspective and insight regarding your life's true purpose.

ROSE-TINTED BATH

To engender love and compassion betwixt yourself and those who may not make it easy, do this.

Soak a lump of rose quartz and a polished pebble of the same rock in cold water at the bottom of the bath for at least an hour, then remove the gemstones, add hot water, and sprinkle six drops of rose oil in the loving brew. Get in, envisaging the water glowing pink and your/their negativity evaporating. Think of interacting in perfect harmony. Relax and enjoy.

When you emerge, continue to visualize yourself glowing with this pink energy. Take the smaller rose quartz, hold it, and transfer your new color into it. It may help to rub it with a little rose oil.

Put the pebble in your pocket when you go out, and hold it in your hand whenever the situation arises. "See" the pink light emanating from the gemstone and recharging you with positivity.

You may like to attempt to transfer this to the other party too.

TOOLS OF ENCHANTMENT

Some of the most psychically effective equipment is the simplest. A cut crystal hung in the window, for example, will shift stale energy with spectrum-color magick. Wind chimes also add magick to the atmosphere and keep negative entities at bay. Both produce harmony in a room or household.

AROMATIC AID

A couple of drops of essential oil in a burner or in the bath will change your day. Choose:

★ **SANDALWOOD** for emotional warmth and magick

★ **YLANG-YLANG AND GERANIUM** for ideas and inspiration

★ **LAVENDER** for mental clarity

★ **FRANKINCENSE** to encourage prosperity

★ **ORANGE** for friendship and happiness

APHRODITE'S REFRESHER

To reinvoke love in a relationship, take alternate sips
with your partner from a silver chalice (or a chalice-
shaped glass) containing fresh strawberry juice and
some halves of the fruit, topped up with
champagne. You will soon find good vibrations
flowing between you again.

ENLIVENING THE CHAKRAS

Light a small rainbow candle and, as it burns, concentrate on each chakra (or energy center) in turn, as follows:

★ **RED:** Base chakra

★ **ORANGE:** Intestinal chakra

★ **YELLOW:** Solar plexus chakra

★ **GREEN:** Heart chakra

★ **BLUE:** Throat chakra

★ **PURPLE:** Third-eye chakra

★ **FLAME:** Crown chakra

You will soon feel psychically refreshed and ready for magick on any plane.

DiViNE NOURISHMENT

Light a yellow candle with a request for health and prosperity. Envisage nourishing golden light flowing from the Universe into the focus of the flame, then into you. When you are sated and glowing, extinguish the flame, and feel yourself emanating its light from every pore. When depleted, repeat.

CHAKRA CLEANSER

Keep a quartz crystal in the water container
you use the most. The longer the crystal
soaks, the stronger the purifying properties
of the water will be. As you drink the
crystal water, feel it cleansing your subtle
and physical bodies, brightening and
energizing your chakras.

YESODIC BOOST

For creative inspiration, imagine you are standing on the snowcapped peak of a purple mountain beneath a harvest moon. Feel the vibrational essence of inner life all around you; allow it to enter your system through the crown of your head and between your eyebrows. When you are ready, return to everyday life. You should find your imaginative capacities greatly enhanced.

KARMIC CALMER

If you are angry and do not wish to be, remove yourself from the situation of emotional toxicity, then breathe in white light and envisage red light exiting your body as you exhale. As you calm down, the light you exhale grows pinker and paler. When the light you exhale is white, it is safe to reenter the fray, resolving to keep your cool.

NO PAIN, NO GAIN

Remember that every discomfort you undergo and every problem you encounter is nullifying your personal karma. Thus nothing, however seemingly pointless, is without its purpose.

Realize that you deserve the best in life because you will use it well, and to the benefit of all.

PSYCHIC ENHANCEMENT

Get a friend to put a mystery object into a box. With your eyes closed, concentrate on your third-eye area and imagine it bathed in violet light. Slowly "open" this eye, and try to "see" what is in the box. Do not think; use intuition only.

For lateral spells and visualizations to increase psychic ability and intuition, and to get to the bottom of emotional depths, work on a Monday. Use jasmine oil or incense, or anything that to you is lunar or ethereal. Suitable props include silver, moonstone, pearl, quartz crystal, and milk.

THE CELTIC TREE CALENDAR

Appealing to those of us with a penchant for nature-spirits, this ancient system catalogs the seasons and their corresponding trees, moods, and energies. Studying the trees concerned deeply enhances perception of each month. Epic poems such as *The Battle of the Trees* amply describe their traits, as perceived in Bardic lore and analyzed in Robert Graves's *White Goddess*, a literary touchstone in every witch's and poet's library.

★ **BETH** (Birch): December 24–January 20

★ **LUIS** (Rowan): January 21– February 17

★ **NION** (Ash): February 18–March 17

★ **FEARN** (Alder): March 18–April 14

★ **SAILLE** (Willow): April 15–May 12

- ★ **UATH** (Hawthorn): May 13–June 9

- ★ **DUIR** (Oak): June 10–July 7

- ★ **TINNE** (Holly): July 8–August 4

- ★ **COLL** (Hazel): August 5–September 1

- ★ **MUIN** (Vine): September 2–
  September 29

- ★ **GORT** (Ivy): September 30–October 27

- ★ **NGETAL** (Reed): October 28–November 24

- ★ **RUIS** (Elder): November 25–December 23

GEBURIC DEFENSES

To overcome enmity and increase personal power, work on a Tuesday. Cedar and tobacco are appropriate fragrances; ritual paraphernalia can be ferrous, red, and symbolically military: magickal daggers and swords, for example (though these are never used to harm, only to channel energy). This is a good day to bless a ritual sword if you have one. If not, try this:

Visualize all of your determination and will to succeed as a long, sharp sword. Envisage the hilt too, the metal of which it is made, and any other suitable details. Concentrate on it until it is completely solid in your mind. Every time you have a battle on your hands, envisage your sword hacking away at any obstacles.

"Clean" your sword regularly by imagining brilliant light flowing through it and dissolving all pollutants. You should find your determination and ability to succeed greatly enhanced.

Travel Tonic

Worried about a journey? A couple of drops of comfrey oil on a blue silk square will help keep fear and peril at bay. A bath beforehand containing a few comfrey leaves will also soothe troubled nerves.

Gods who specialize in helping travelers include the Greek god Hermes, and Anubis, the Egyptian jackal-headed god. Concentrating on them and asking that you be guided safely to your destination may also help.

FOR MENTAL ALERTNESS

For issues of academe, communication, ritual, and
business scenarios, Wednesday gives the optimum
influences. Lavender is mentally bracing, and eight
drops burned in a censer will work wonders.
Shower rather than bathe. Use the caduceus symbol
(two snakes wrapped around a staff) to help focus
your mind.

QUICK BOOSTER VISUALIZATION

Lacking in energy? Go outside, preferably somewhere fresh and in sunlight, and take several deep lungfuls of the air.

As you inhale, envisage the bright prana, or life-energy, entering your lungs until they glow. Now "see" that light being absorbed through your lungs into your bloodstream, coursing around your body, bringing refreshment and clean energy to your system.

Ritual Tools

Candles and incense are important ritual tools because they can hone the mind to a very specific goal if selected appropriately. Other classical witches' tools include the athame, or black-handled knife; the boline, which is white-handled and curved and used for harvesting herbs; the chalice; and sometimes the ritual sword, for channeling energy. None of these implements is ever used to cause harm, but they are all helpful symbols.

Real magick happens when a mind interacts with the Universe and impresses its Will on the subtle energies that determine our lives. The essential ritual tools for any witch are therefore the ability to visualize creatively and the determination and enthusiasm to succeed.

URBANE
INSPIRATION

If you've got the urban blues, a (carefully
tended) midnight bonfire will chill and thrill
the harassed Pagan within. Or wax lyrical by
candlelight with friends and children in
Druidic style, expelling the smog from
the lungs of the city-clogged Bard
with saga and song.

THOUGHT-FORMS

Remember that whatever you imagine becomes real on the astral plane. If envisaged frequently enough, it may take on a form and energy of its own. Positive thoughts are of infinitely more benefit than negative ones, which pollute the aura and may cause all kinds of unpleasantness. Create a repository of strength by establishing an astral container (in whatever form you wish) for happiness and inspiration when you feel it. This container can become a point of psychic pilgrimage, helping you to maintain equilibrium when the chips are down.

AN AROMATIC ANTIDOTE
TO CIGARETTE CRAVINGS

Lavender oil can help you quit smoking. A room full of evaporated lavender is healthier and more fragrant than toxic tobacco, and lavender really helps diminish the urge to smoke. Try it!

THE POWER OF CONVICTION

If you really want something (within reason), imagine that you already have it. The surer you are that it "belongs" to you, the more magnetic will you become to that object or situation. The stronger your visualization and imagining that you have what you desire, the surer you are of success. So choose your desires carefully!

DIVINATION BY
FIRE, AIR, AND EARTH

For powers of prophecy, burn a miniature Fire of
Azrael (as a divining fire is known) by using cedar
chips, juniper, and sandalwood on a charcoal disk.
What can you see in the flames, and what do the
shapes in the smoke symbolize to you?

TO ATTRACT THE APPLE OF YOUR EYE

Unrequited love? Eat a red apple in the vicinity of your beloved, then plant the core during a waxing moon, saying:

Seeds of love, grow strong
and blossom.

Visualize the other person's love taking root in you, just as the apple's seeds take root in the earth. Imagine his or her growth and pleasure being sustained by your interaction as the apple was eaten. Soon the Venusian allure will take effect.

PSYCHIC
SELF-PROTECTION

For psychic self-protection, envisage yourself at the center of a tongue of blue fire. Within this psychic flame you are inviolate. Approaching detrimental forces are instantly incinerated, but beneficial ones are absorbed and add luster to your light. The light, burning superbright, sends shades and shadows packing in the astral realms. Thus you are at once protected and a living luminary.

GENTLE EXORCISM

To rid a home or room of unwanted influences,
place some salt in water in the North-West of a
room, incense in the East, and a bell and candle in
the South. Walking clockwise, ring the bell, flick a
little of the salt water, and waft the incense, saying:

Sorrows past be gone.
Love and light stay long.

ASTRAL ARMOR
(SEE ALSO PSYCHIC SELF-PROTECTION ON PAGE 150)

For double psychic protection in times of crisis,
imagine that the aura-flame is a fluid suit of armor.
You can check its durability by mentally bouncing an
attack off its surface. "See" and feel the virulent
words/emotions/thoughts rebounding from it and
returning to their sender. (If you are feeling kind,
you could visualize them being sent into the earth.)
Know that your suit of astral armor will let none of
the slings and arrows of outrageous colleagues/
partners/family members in, and that your
callousness to their entreaty or attack is complete.

FEELS SEW RIGHT

Making your own garment to wear in ritual is a great way of focusing your energy and committing to a successful rhythm of witchcraft. Robes and light shifts are traditional, practical, and easy to make. A sewing machine will help, but use only natural materials such as cotton, and hand-stitch the last part of the garment in order to imbue it with your intent to be a respectful, proficient, and powerful witch.

RUNE-BLESSING SPELL

Most of us have a set of runes. My own were made of applewood (from Chalice Orchard in Glastonbury) by a wonderful Arch Druid friend. He also made some of blackthorn for a friend. Such special tools require a special blessing, so I wrote poems for each rune, incorporating its meaning. Try writing your own devotional verses while you focus on each rune individually. You can learn them, chant them, even sing them if you have the pitch for it. (Each rune has its own musical wavelength.) For example:

FEYU RUNE CHANT

Fuel for needfire, grain to spare,
Plenteous gifts from Vanir fair.
Open-armed, we greet and share
The natural bounty of Freya and Freyr.
And when the field abounds with beast,
In coming winter shall we feast,
Dodging raid and plightful battle
By boasting not of plenteous cattle.

For fortune fickle and serpent's spit
Into the FEYU rune are writ!

HOUSEHOLD PROTECTION

Rosemary will cleanse evil influences and avert the evil eye. Sage and mint purify and protect. Grow these near your front and back doors to help maintain a healthy, happy household.

GLIMPSING THE VANISHING PEOPLE

Don't believe in fairies? On Beltane or Midsummer's Eve at twilight, sit in a natural setting and entwine seven inches of red ribbon with two ribbons of green around the stem of an oak, hawthorn, or spindle tree. As you do so, sense the elemental interest your act engenders.

Soon you should perceive the peer of elfin eyes on your enterprise, tingling in your fingers, and tip-tapping at your sensitive spine. Allow your intuition to roam the subtler plane, and you will not be blinkered by disbelief again.

The easiest way to ruin magickal work is to talk about it, so Know, Will, Dare, and BE SILENT!

THE LiTTLE BOOK OF POCKET SPELLS

Andrews McMeel Publishing
a division of Andrews McMeel Universal
1130 Walnut Street, Kansas City, Missouri 64106

www.andrewsmcmeel.com

19 20 21 22 23 TEN 10 9 8 7 6 5 4 3 2

ISBN: 978-1-4494-9577-0

Library of Congress Control Number: 2018938603

ATTENTiON: SCHOOLS AND BUSiNESSES

Andrews McMeel books are available at quantity
discounts with bulk purchase for educational, business,
or sales promotional use. For information, please e-mail the
Andrews McMeel Publishing Special Sales Department:
specialsales@amuniversal.com.